THIS IS A WORKBOOK FOR BREAKING FREE FROM BROKE:

A PRACTICAL GUIDE TO MAKE MORE MONEY AND LESS STRESS.

©

GARDEN PRINTS

This Workbook is dedicated
to anyone who wishes to
earn money.

APPLYING THIS WORKBOOK:

1. Gather your writing tools.

2. Fill in the blanks with any thoughts that spring to mind.

3. Make sure you apply all you've learned in this workbook.

OWNER:

D. O. B:

JOB:

This is an independent workbook for George Kamel's Breaking Free From Broke that covers every major detail of the book.

It's no longer news how we have a lot poorer people these days and this epidemic of poverty just keeps on growing. It's turning to a viscous circle. If you truly yearn to break out of this circle, then this workbook is for you.

THE FIRST STEP

"GET A JOB."

If you want to earn big in life you need to get a job. Although, this quite simple. But a lot of people spend time planning and at the end of the day, they have plans and dreams that may never be implemented because these days almost every dream needs the adequate funding. So this is a subtle but firm reminder to get up your butt and work for some cash.

HOW SHOULD IT BE DONE?

Try looking for jobs that
work for you.

TIPS

I understand you're looking
for money but understand
the job description before
you leap so you aren't
saddened with regrets in the
long run.

WORTH NOTING

THE SECOND STEP

"REFINE YOUR SKILLS."

What are the use of skills when you can't use them? It would just seem pointless right? A lot of people these days get skills but they left it tucked in on a shelf and let technology roll right pass them and these skills became obsolete.

These days getting skills is not just enough you need to sharpen them every once in a while else the world would just move right past you. People are always willing to pay for value but you need to be off value yourself.

HOW SHOULD IT BE DONE?

Try taking classes online.

TIPS

Pride usually comes before a fall. When you feel you know everything, you can never really get what you want in life because there's no one person that truly knows everything.

WORTHY OF MENTION

THE THIRD STEP

"PLAN ACCORDINGLY."

Working is important but it's not enough. You need proper structure set in plan and this can only come when you plan properly. You need to see SMART GOALS for yourself so you are working with a clear picture of your target/ goal in mind. Your goals must be specific, measurable, attainable, relevant and time based. If your goals can't be vetted this way, then you most likely haven't started.

HOW SHOULD IT BE DONE?

Create a comprehensive vision board that comprises of your short, medium and long-term goals so you can become more accountable, consistent and time conscious.

TIPS

Always have a backup plan.

WORTH NOTING

THE FOURTH STEP

"WORK SMART NOT HARD."

One of the blessings of this generation is that a lot of have really come to understand the tenets of smart work. It takes you a step further.

Sometimes it's sad how you work long and hard but it might not really be rewarding. A lot of people work long hours like first line managers in a company. They are the muscle of the company but they don't earn as much as the executives.

HOW SHOULD IT BE DONE?

Planning and picking the right career for yourself is the perfect place to start.

TIPS

Working smart simply requires you to work with your brains rather than brawn.

WORTH NOTING

_____

_____

_____

_____

_____

_____

_____

_____

_____

_____

_____

_____

_____

_____

_____

_____

_____

_____

_____

THE FIFTH STEP

"SAVE."

It's as good a plan as any to learn the importance of saving and early too. When you have proper strategy in play and you don't know the importance of saving up for the future you want, you are an impulsive spender, then I hate to be the one to break it to you but chances are you might probably be broke for a while. You need to understand the rule of saving and investments for the future.

HOW SHOULD IT BE DONE?

Set up a proper savings account and start small.

TIPS

Saving is like an investment for rainy days.

WORTH NOTING

SIXTH STEP

"MONETIZE YOUR HOBBIES."

Hobbies are simply things you love doing. They are usually part of your definition of your happy place, your comfort zone even. Hobbies can range from designing, writing, painting to even coding. But hobbies don't need to be just that. Imagine doing what you love and getting paid for it, that's the dream.

HOW SHOULD IT BE DONE?

Try advertising these
hobbies for a start.

TIPS

This could become the
thrust into your dream life.

WORTH NOTING

SEVENTH STEP

"REDUCE YOUR SCREENTIME."

Definitely, this would make the list. I'm pretty sure you've heard it a thousand times that you need to reduce your screen time and it is just as important here.

If you're being honest with yourself, you can attest to the fact that scrolling through your social media accounts like Instagram or Twitter takes longer time than you estimated. This is because social media can be a vortex at times.

HOW SHOULD IT BE DONE?

Set timers on each app so you don't spend too much time on the internet or on your phone in general.

TIPS

Remember, reduction not elimination. The Internet can also help you learn latest trends in your industry.

WORTH NOTING

EIGHTH STEP

"GET FUNDING."

A lot of people have had good dreams but gave up on them because of lack of funding. Don't let that happen to you.

Saving is important but sponsorships would also go a long way. Don't see it as begging for help but making use of an open door.

HOW SHOULD IT BE DONE?

Try pitching your ideas for friends, family and keep an eye open for government sponsorship.

TIPS

Do not get desperate and get a loan. It's never worth it.

WORTH NOTING

NINTH STEP

"GET SLEEP."

I have heard the popular myth that when you sleep, you can't never make it because it shows that you're lazy but I beg to differ. Just know when to strike a balance. Working late all the time reduces your brain speed eventually so do not be too quick to trade your night's rest.

HOW SHOULD IT BE DONE?

Get a good sleep regimen.

TIPS

For better brain activity, out
need to sleep at least six
hours every night.

WORTH NOTING

_____
_____
_____
_____
_____
_____
_____
_____
_____
_____
_____
_____
_____
_____
_____
_____
_____
_____
_____

THE TENTH STEP

"DOWNTIME AND SELF-CARE."

Although it seems really minimalistic and off point, when trying to work for money you need to create some time for yourself where your brain can relax and unplug.

HOW SHOULD IT BE DONE?

Try scheduling off days a least once a week or thrice a month.

TIPS

All work and no play makes Jack a dull boy.

WORTH NOTING

WE HAVE COMPLETED THIS WORKBOOK.

AFTER OBSERVING THE ABOVE STEPS, YOU WILL CERTAINLY MAKE A DIFFERENCE IN YOUR LIFE!

IS THIS WORKBOOK USEFUL FOR YOU?

NOTES ON INSPIRATION

OTHER THINGS TO NOTE

Made in United States
Troutdale, OR
11/27/2024

25372403R00024